Mysterious You

Zzz....

The most interesting book you'll ever read about sleep

Written by Trudee Romanek

Illustrated by Rose Cowles

Kids Can Press

Tremendous thanks are due to Dr. James MacFarlane of the Centre for Sleep and Chronobiology in Toronto for his invaluable review of this book. Thanks also to Dr. Claudio Stampi, director of Boston's Chronobiology Research Institute, Dr. J. J. Lipsitz and the Sleep Disorders Centre of Metropolitan Toronto, and the many sleep scientists who have given up countless nights of sleep in the name of research. And finally, I am grateful to editors Linda Biesenthal and Val Wyatt for their patience and guidance, and to Rose Cowles, whose artwork truly brings a book to life.

Kids Can Press acknowledges the financial support of the Ontario Arts Council, the Canada Council for the Arts and the Government of Canada, through the BPIDP, for our publishing activity.

Published in Canada by
Kids Can Press Ltd.
29 Birch Avenue
Toronto, ON M4V 1E2

Published in the U.S. by
Kids Can Press Ltd.
2250 Military Road
Tonawanda, NY 14150

www.kidscanpress.com

Edited by Linda Biesenthal and Valerie Wyatt
Designed by Marie Bartholomew
Printed in Hong Kong by Wing King Tong Company Limited

The hardcover edition of this book is smyth sewn casebound.
The paperback edition of this book is limp sewn with a drawn-on cover.

CM 02 0 9 8 7 6 5 4 3 2 1
CM PA 02 0 9 8 7 6 5 4 3 2 1

National Library of Canada Cataloguing in Publication Data

Romanek, Trudee
   Zzz...: the most interesting book you'll ever read about sleep

(Mysterious you)
Includes index.

ISBN 1-55074-944-7 (bound)   ISBN 1-55074-946-3 (pbk.)

1. Sleep — Juvenile literature. I. Cowles, Rose, 1967– II. Title. III. Series: Mysterious you (Toronto, Ont.)

QP425.R64 2002   j612.8'21   C2001-901747-2

Kids Can Press is a Nelvana company

Contents

Sleep for Life

It's 3 A.M. on May 20, 1927, and Charles Lindbergh can't sleep. In a few hours, the daring pilot will take off from New York, hoping to become the first person to fly solo across the Atlantic Ocean. But without a good night's sleep, will he be able to stay alert during the 30-hour flight to Paris?

When his plane takes off just before 8 A.M., Lindbergh has had no sleep for 24 hours. As night falls, he struggles to stay awake and has to use his fingers to hold his eyes open. After 50 hours without sleep, even the thrill of the flight can't keep Lindbergh awake. He nods off and his plane flies out of control. Suddenly, the pilot wakes — just in time to avoid crashing into the ocean. Almost 60 hours since he last slept, Lindbergh spots the Paris airfield and prepares to land.

Lindbergh was lucky to make it safely to Paris. Like you, even famous pilots need sleep. Sleep gives your body a chance to grow and repair itself, and it keeps your brain alert so you can think straight. Sleep is one of life's necessities — you can't survive without it.

I must stay awake. I must stay awake. I must . . .

- Weightlifters who were allowed only three hours of sleep one night couldn't lift as much weight the next day.

- When your body is trying to heal itself, your cells release a substance to make you sleepy. Even recovering from a sunburn can make you sleep more.

- Tests show that when a person stays up until 3 A.M., the next day their body has 30 percent fewer "natural killer cells" — the cells that fight viruses.

Losing Sleep

Strange things start to happen when you don't get the sleep you need. Losing just two hours sleep in one night can affect how alert you are and how well you do things the next day. After one full night without sleep, you might have a hard time choosing the right words when you speak. You'd begin to feel worried and depressed. Your judgment and ability to make decisions wouldn't be as good. Your memory would begin to fail, and you'd have a hard time concentrating. You'd take twice as long as usual to react to things, and your body would have difficulty fighting off infections. Whew! And all because you missed just one night's sleep.

Super Sleeper

Ever heard the story of Rip Van Winkle? One evening while hunting, Rip lay down and fell asleep. He awoke to find his rifle covered in rust and his chin covered in a long beard. It turns out he'd been asleep for 20 years. Believe it or not, you will sleep for 20 years, too — just not all at once!

Sleep is so important that we spend a third of each day doing it. That's almost 3000 hours, or more than four months, each year. And that means if you live to be 70 years old, you'll spend about 23 years sleeping — more than Rip Van Winkle himself.

Are You Sleeping?

In 1976, researchers at Stanford University allowed a volunteer to sleep just four hours one night. The next day, they asked him to lie on a bed with his eyes taped open. They placed a bright light just 15 cm (6 in.) above his face and flashed it every few seconds. The volunteer was to tap a switch whenever he saw the light flash. For several minutes, he tapped the switch after each flash. Then, after one flash, he did nothing. When the researchers asked him why he hadn't tapped the switch, the volunteer said the light had not flashed. The man had become so tired that, without realizing it, he simply fell asleep for a few seconds with his eyes open.

When you're awake, you notice things around you because your brain is responding to messages from your senses. You hear the radio playing, smell dinner cooking, feel cool air on your skin. And you remember most things that happen. Being asleep is a different story. Think about it. Do you remember if it rained last night, or how many times you rolled over in your sleep? Probably not. When you're sleeping, your brain doesn't react to all the messages from your senses, and you're not nearly as aware of what's happening around you.

Red Alert!!

You're sound asleep when suddenly a screeching sound jolts you wide awake. It's the smoke alarm. But if your brain isn't aware of things around you as you sleep, how did the noise wake you? Although you may not remember hearing other, quieter sounds, your ears did sense them. It's just that the messages your ears sent reached only part of your brain. That part decided the sound wasn't important enough to interrupt your sleep. Loud sounds that could mean danger, however, usually get your whole brain's attention and wake you up.

- On May 17, 1928, Alvin "Shipwreck" Kelly climbed to a platform the size of a dinner plate at the top of a flagpole in Louisville, Kentucky. He was determined to perch there for 100 hours. Doctors warned that he would drift off to sleep and fall, but somehow Alvin managed to last for a full four days and eight hours.

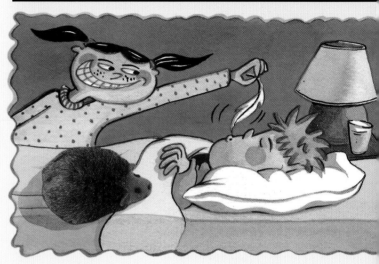

You Try It

Remember the fairy-tale princess who slept poorly because of a pea under her mattress? Like the princess, most sleepers react to things that bother them while they sleep. Ask your brother (or someone else) if you can try these tests on him 15 minutes after he falls asleep. Or have him try them on you.

- Gently place a tennis ball under his back. He will likely change position without waking up. That's because the uncomfortable pressure of the ball sends a message to part of his brain without waking the rest of it.

- Gently touch his face with a feather or piece of string. Did he try to brush it away without rousing from sleep?

Feeling Sleepy?

It's been a busy day. An hour before bedtime, you start feeling sleepy and begin to yawn. Your temperature drops a few tenths of a degree. Your body is gearing down for its nightly rest.

Once in bed, you relax. You may feel as though you are falling, or your body may suddenly jerk. You may "see" things that aren't there and hear voices. These are hypnagogic (hip-nuh-GAW-jik) hallucinations. They occur as you cross the line between wakefulness and sleep. Then after about 20 minutes — click! You enter the mysterious land of sleep.

Inside the Sleeping Brain

Once you're asleep, your brain stem — the part that looks after your body's automatic systems — slows down your breathing, heart rate, digestion and urine production. But the brain itself changes when you're sleeping, too.

Your brain produces different kinds of electrical activity — called "brainwaves" — depending on what you're doing. Your "asleep" brainwaves are different from those your brain produces when you're awake.

Experts can tell the moment a person falls asleep just by looking at the changes in the pattern of the brainwaves recorded by a machine called an electroencephalograph (EEG). Take a look at the brainwave recording below. The red circle marks the point when this person fell asleep.

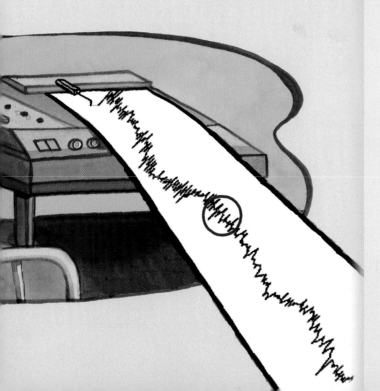

Yawn!

Like a sneeze, a yawn happens whether you want it to or not. A yawn makes you open your mouth wide and take a slow, deep breath. Your lungs expand with air, and your jaw muscles stretch to hold your mouth open for about six seconds.

The deep breath sends more oxygen to your body and especially to your brain. It also helps clear out carbon dioxide, the gas we breathe out. That may be why you yawn, although scientists aren't quite sure.

Mostly, people yawn just before bed or when they wake up, but just thinking about yawning can make you yawn. You may even be yawning while you're reading this! And when one person yawns, people nearby may yawn, too. Try yawning a few times during dinner. Did you get anyone else at the table yawning?

The Body's Clock

Ever wondered what makes you sleepy at bedtime? Is it just that you're tired out from a long day? That may be part of it, but you also get tired because your brain tells you to. A tiny part of each person's brain controls at what time of the day you'll feel wide awake and what time you'll feel sleepy.

People call this part of the brain the biological clock, or the body clock. Of course, it's not really a clock. It's actually two tiny clumps of nerve cells — about the size of two pinheads — inside your brain. The real name of these clumps of cells is the suprachiasmatic nuclei (SOO-pra-ki-az-MAT-ik NOO-klee-i), or the SCN for short. They help your brain produce the right chemicals, called neurotransmitters and hormones, to make you feel sleepy as bedtime gets nearer and ready to rise as morning approaches.

- Milk, turkey and some other foods contain an amino acid called tryptophan that's related to serotonin, a neurotransmitter that makes you sleepy. But eating these foods won't make you sleepy unless you consume huge amounts — like 20 to 30 glasses of milk!

Putting the Brain to Sleep

During the day, your biological clock triggers your body to produce chemicals that stimulate your brain and keep it alert. While it's alert, a part of your brain stem — the lower part of your brain that looks after breathing and other basic life functions — is hard at work. It passes information non-stop from your senses to your cerebral cortex — the upper part of your brain that sorts out information from your senses and controls speech and all your other muscle movements.

Later, your biological clock signals your body that bedtime is approaching. When the daylight begins to fade, your pineal gland churns out more melatonin, a hormone that lets your organs know it's time for sleep. Your brain starts producing less of the stimulating, wake-up chemicals. Eventually, another part of the brain stem (the pontine nuclei) takes over, allowing you to sleep. Once this part is in charge, very little sensory information is passed to your cerebral cortex and you are no longer as aware of things around you.

The brain stem itself doesn't seem to need sleep. It may be the part of your brain that stays alert during sleep, waiting for important signals.

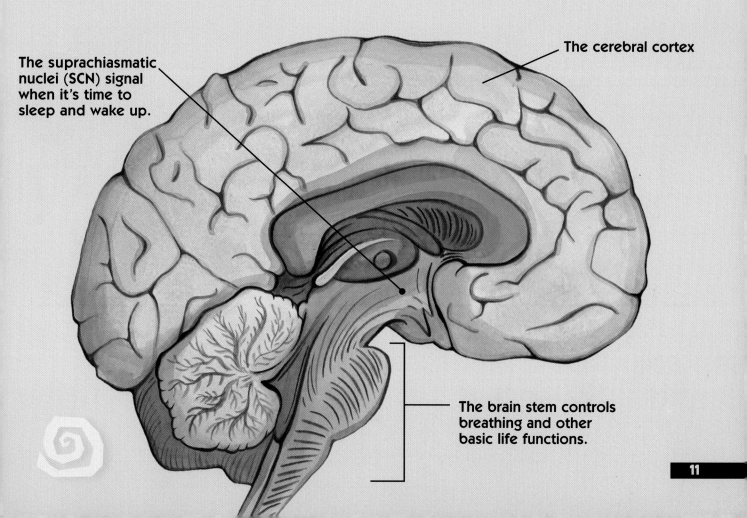

The suprachiasmatic nuclei (SCN) signal when it's time to sleep and wake up.

The cerebral cortex

The brain stem controls breathing and other basic life functions.

Right on Time

People are creatures of habit, thanks in part to their biological clocks. Scientists have discovered that, over the course of each day, human beings (and other animals, too) have a distinct pattern of times when they are sleepy and times when they are alert. Most people feel energetic in the morning, then start to feel sleepy after lunch. They perk up in late afternoon, feel wide awake right after supper and then get tired at bedtime. This sleep/wake cycle is part of a larger, 24-hour pattern called the circadian rhythm.

Some other events in your day are part of your circadian rhythm as well. For example, your body temperature rises just before you wake up and falls during the night. And your stomach produces digestive juices according to a schedule, so that at meal times it's ready to break down the food you eat.

9–11 A.M.

1–4 P.M.

6–8 P.M.

Gathering Evidence

Your biological clock uses a number of different clues to make sure it's keeping your circadian rhythm on schedule. Eating and exercising at regular times, even brushing your teeth and putting on your pajamas before bed can signal your brain that everything is happening when it's supposed to. But the most important time clue for your biological clock is daylight.

When your eyes sense light, optical fibers carry the message to your brain and your SCN. As long as your eyes are sensing bright light during the day and no light at night, your biological clock knows that it's waking you up, making you sleepy and triggering all those other events at the correct times.

1–4 A.M.

Flowers that Tell Time

Researchers have found that almost every living thing — animals, insects and even bacteria and fungi — has a biological clock that structures its day and night. Bees, for example, only gather nectar from flowers at a certain time of the day. Even plants often have a daily schedule.

In 1748, a Swedish scientist named Carolus Linnaeus planted a sort of garden clock. Each kind of plant in his garden opened or closed its flowers at a different, specific time of day. Linnaeus could tell what time it was just by looking at which flowers were open.

Turning Day into Night

Many animals, including humans, are diurnal — awake and active during the day. These days, though, many businesses are open 24 hours. Employees on night shift have to sleep during the day instead. This can cause big problems.

If you switched night for day and day for night long enough, your body might get used to the change. The problem is that most shiftworkers don't stick to the new schedule for long, so their bodies don't have time to adjust. As a result shiftworkers often feel sleepy at work, but lie awake in bed when they're supposed to be sleeping.

Sleepy Heads

Air traffic controllers at a Los Angeles airport were surprised when the crew of an approaching jet didn't answer their radio calls. Then, instead of turning to land, the jet continued straight toward the Pacific Ocean. The reason? It was flying on autopilot because the entire flight crew had fallen asleep! The jet flew 165 km (100 mi.) off course before someone in the control tower set off an alarm in the cockpit and woke the crew.

Flying from one time zone to another can throw your body into a tailspin. Suddenly the hours between sunrise and sunset don't add up to a complete day. The more time zones you cross, the more out of whack your biological clock gets. Your brain may produce chemicals that keep you wide awake when everyone else is asleep. It can take a week before daylight resets your clock and gets all the systems of your circadian rhythm back to normal.

- In space, astronauts sometimes face their most difficult tasks when they would normally be sleeping back on Earth. So, before a mission, NASA shines bright lights on the astronauts in the middle of the night to reset their biological clocks.

Getting off Schedule

Many teenagers have a problem called teenage phase shift. Even though their bodies are growing a lot, they don't produce more melatonin — the chemical that signals it's time for bed. So the melatonin signal is weaker, and they don't feel sleepy until well after midnight. Getting up is a nightmare, and they drag themselves around exhausted for the rest of the day. By evening, they're wide awake again and can't get to sleep. To deal with the problem of sleepy teens, some U.S. high schools are starting classes later in the morning so that students can get the sleep they need.

Stages of Sleep

In 1952, American researcher Nathaniel Kleitman began studying the eyes of sleepers. He knew that our eyes roll around slowly just as we're falling asleep. But he didn't know if this happened at other times during the night as well.

Kleitman asked a research student, Eugene Aserinsky, to stay awake all night and watch a sleeping person's eyes. Aserinsky was astonished by what he saw. Although the sleeper's eyeballs didn't roll, from time to time they darted very quickly back and forth under closed eyelids. What Kleitman and Aserinsky had discovered was a special stage of sleep. They named it Rapid Eye Movement (REM) sleep and soon found that it's during REM sleep that sleepers have their most elaborate dreams.

Sleep researchers everywhere began to monitor brainwaves throughout the whole night. What they found was that the brainwaves changed during the night, not just once, but many times. They divided the different types of brainwaves into five stages of sleep that people go through each night — REM sleep and stages 1, 2, 3 and 4 of non-REM sleep.

- **Almost all mammals have periods of light and deep sleep and periods of REM sleep, but researchers can't detect the two clear patterns of REM and non-REM sleep in reptiles.**

Non-REM Sleep

Stage 1 sleep is so close to being awake that if you were woken from it you'd probably say you weren't even asleep. After several minutes in Stage 1, you sink into Stage 2 sleep. The brainwaves during this stage are a little larger and slower than at Stage 1. From there you sink into the deeper sleep of Stages 3 and 4. Your body is very relaxed and it is difficult to wake you. During Stage 4, your body produces the largest amount of some of the chemicals that help you grow.

Stages 1 and 2 are often called light sleep. Stages 3 and 4 are called deep sleep, or Slow-Wave Sleep (SWS), because your brainwaves are larger and slower in those stages.

Asleep in the Snow?

If you think hibernating animals just snooze through the winter, think again. When scientists monitored the brainwaves of some hibernators, they discovered that the animals didn't produce any brainwaves at all for most of the time. Every few weeks, though, the brainwave monitoring showed that the animals did drift up from hibernation into sleep for a couple of hours before sinking back into a hibernation state again.

Most experts think that animals hibernate to slow their bodies' systems so that they can survive with less food during the snowy season when there is less to eat.

The Sleep Cycle

Throughout the night, you make your way through the five stages of sleep on a very regular schedule. After falling asleep, you drift down through light sleep (Stages 1 and 2) and then into deep SWS sleep (Stages 3 and 4). You stay in Stage 4 sleep for about 20 minutes, your longest chunk of it for the night. Then, you begin to drift back up through Stage 3 and into the lighter sleep of Stage 2. But instead of passing into Stage 1 and then waking up, you enter your first period of REM (rapid eye movement) sleep.

For the rest of the night you pass up and down through the stages of sleep in cycles that last a little more than an hour. You spend less time in deep SWS and more time in REM sleep as the night passes. In fact, most people have no deep sleep at all after about 2 A.M.

- Most small mammals have shorter sleep cycles than larger mammals. A mouse passes through its sleep cycle in nine minutes, an elephant takes as long as two hours.

Sleeping like a Baby

Newborn babies don't seem to have much of a sleep cycle. They sleep for an hour or two, wake up for a while and then fall asleep again — no matter what time of day it is. Even though they sleep so much, most babies don't get any deep sleep (Stage 3 or 4) at all until they're about three months old. Instead, they spend half of their sleep time in Stages 1 and 2 of light sleep and the other half — around eight hours each day — in REM sleep. Babies get this large amount of REM sleep at the time their brains are developing the most. Some scientists think REM sleep somehow helps the brain develop. By the age of three, children spend only a quarter of their sleep time in REM sleep, about the same amount as an adult.

You can recognize the rapid eye movements of REM sleep in someone else — or in a pet. Watch a cat or dog while it is sleeping (but don't disturb it). Check the pet after it's been asleep for 10 to 20 minutes. Can you see its eyeballs darting back and forth under its eyelids?

How long did the REM period last? The pet may growl or twitch its ears or paws as it dreams. Did your sleeper move any other part of its body during that time?

Sweet Dreams

You're at the Olympic Games. The crowd cheers as you kneel at the starting line of the 100-meter dash. You check out the competition and see Bluebeard the Pirate crouched in one lane and your pet goldfish in another. As the starting gun fires, you realize something — a dozen television crews are filming you.

Sound strange? Not if you know it's a dream — one of those strange stories your brain makes up while you're in REM sleep. Everyone dreams. Most people dream for about an hour every night during REM sleep. We dream in other stages of sleep, too, but those dreams are about fairly normal things, and people seem to forget those more easily. Some people don't remember any of their dreams at all. And although people dream in color, some only remember the dream adventures in black and white. Color seems to be the first thing to fade from memory.

- We dream what we see. Researchers asked volunteers to wear goggles with red-tinted lenses 24 hours a day. Each morning, the volunteers described their dreams. Within a few days all the dream objects they reported were red.

The Dreamer's Body

While you're in non-REM sleep, you are relaxed and calm. But your body seems to switch to high alert when you enter REM sleep. Your heart and breathing may suddenly speed up. Your eyes dart around as though you're "watching" your dream take place. Your brainwaves look a lot like they do when you're awake. In fact, your whole body behaves much like it does when you're awake, with one very big difference — you can't move. At all. Your closed eyes dart around and you may twitch a little, but you never move. You are paralyzed. Unless something very scary or startling happens in a dream that shocks you awake, you lie perfectly still until your dream is over. This is called REM sleep paralysis, or atonia.

While you're sleeping, your brain sends messages to your arms and legs to move, just like when you're awake. But in REM sleep, something keeps those messages from reaching their destination. Atonia prevents you from acting out what's happening in your dream. It may also be why some dreamers feel rooted to the spot.

You Try It

Try these tips to help you remember your dreams. Be sure to have a pen and paper beside your bed.

1. Before you go to sleep, tell yourself you're going to have a dream and you're going to remember it.

2. When you wake up, lie quietly for a few minutes and see what thoughts enter your head. Write down any dream snippets you remember.

3. A few times during the day, read over the snippets. Write down any new dream details that you remember.

Why We Dream

If you were sick thousands of years ago in ancient Greece, you might have visited a dream oracle for advice on how to get better. The oracle would perform a ceremony and then put you to bed on a specially prepared sheepskin. When you awoke, you'd describe your dream, and the oracle would figure out what the symbols in your dream meant and declare the cure for your illness.

Through the ages, people have had many different ideas about why we dream. The people of ancient India believed that dreams let them glimpse the world they would go to after they died. And the Senoi people in the jungles of Malaysia used to believe that their dreams warned them of problems or conflicts so that they could avoid them.

Scientists still don't know for sure why we dream, but they have some ideas. One theory is that dreams may be a form of exercise that helps the brain develop.

You must drink more water

- Birds may dream, too! Bird brainwaves indicate that they go into REM sleep, but only for five or six seconds. Still, that may be long enough to dream. When researchers played a recording of birds singing for some "dreaming" birds, the area of their brain that controls singing generated a lot of electrical signals — as if the birds were dreaming about singing back.

Dreaming and Memory

You've been working at your computer for two hours. Your project is half done. Just to be safe, you hit the "save" command before continuing. The computer begins transferring information from the file you've been working on into its permanent memory. Dreaming could be your brain's way of doing exactly what your computer just did.

Some scientists believe that your short-term memory — the part that lets you remember things for a day or so — holds all the new information during the day. Then at night, as you dream, your brain sifts through the day's experiences. It stores the important details in your long-term memory and tosses out the rest, perhaps straight into your dreams.

Scientists haven't yet found a way to prove this theory, but one thing is certain — dreaming IS important. If you are prevented from dreaming, your brain makes up for it by getting extra dream sleep the first chance it can.

You Try It

Next time you remember part of a dream, try to figure out if any of the details came from something that happened that day. Maybe the gorilla on a skateboard came from zoo pictures you saw in the newspaper and the new skateboard you've been wanting. Or maybe you dreamed you were bald because you noticed that a friend got a haircut.

What Dreams Mean

One night in 1865, the German chemist Friedrich Kekulé was trying to figure out the shape and structure of the chemical benzene. Frustrated, he settled into his chair for a nap and dreamed of a snake with its tail in its mouth. When he woke up, he realized his dream held the answer — the molecules of benzene form a ring.

Many creative people say they find inspiration in dreams. The eighteenth-century composer Wolfgang Amadeus Mozart claimed that the music he composed was music he heard in his dreams. After he woke up, he simply wrote down the notes.

Do all dreams, like those of Mozart and Kekulé, hold some important information for the dreamer? Or are dreams really just random thoughts? Some scientists suggest that the electric energy buzzing around inside your head as you sleep happens to stimulate certain areas of your brain, bringing random details to mind. Your dreams may be the stories your brain creates by joining these details together. Is this true? No one knows for sure.

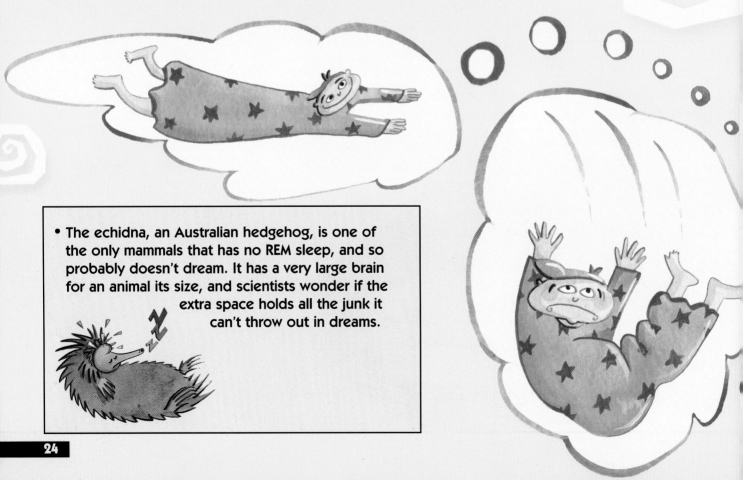

• The echidna, an Australian hedgehog, is one of the only mammals that has no REM sleep, and so probably doesn't dream. It has a very large brain for an animal its size, and scientists wonder if the extra space holds all the junk it can't throw out in dreams.

It's All in Your Head

In 1900, a German doctor named Sigmund Freud published his famous book, **The Interpretation of Dreams**. He was the first person to suggest that the details and events in a dream might have a deeper meaning. For instance, if you dream of yelling at a small, white dog, it could be because you're angry with someone who is short and blond. Freud believed that by analyzing dreams, he could help people recognize feelings they didn't know they had.

What an object or event in a dream means, Freud and others said, depends a lot on the person dreaming it. Still, there are some standard dream symbols that many people apply to their dreams. If you dream of:

- flying, you feel confident
- falling, it could mean you are worried about failing, perhaps at school
- being naked, you may be feeling helpless or self-conscious about something
- a king and queen, they may represent your parents
- a road or path, it may be a symbol of your journey through life

Things that Go Bump in the Night

Long ago, many people thought bad dreams were caused by visits from an evil spirit. That's where the word "nightmare" comes from — in Old English, "mare" means demon.

People of all ages have nightmares, but we dream our scariest ones when we are three or four years old. Experts think this is because that's when our imaginations are forming, and we may have trouble telling what's real from what's not real. For some reason, girls have more nightmares than boys.

Most nightmares occur during the second half of the night, when we are getting more REM sleep. In a nightmare, you feel threatened and in danger. REM sleep paralysis (see page 21) can make a scary nightmare even scarier, because you feel you can't move a muscle to protect yourself. If the fright is strong enough, it may break through the paralysis, allowing you to move. That's why you usually remember the most frightening nightmares — your fear was great enough to wake you up. Most experts think people have nightmares when they are afraid of, or worried about, something.

- Kids sometimes have a kind of bad dream called a night terror. They sit up and scream in fear, but even though their eyes are wide open, they're really still asleep. After several minutes, the fear passes and the sleeper usually just lies back down to sleep — and remembers nothing about it in the morning.

Acting out Dreams

A man dreams he's a football player who's running, jumping and dodging other players. When he wakes up, he finds his bedroom furniture is broken in pieces all around him. Like a small number of others, mostly men over 50, this man has what's called REM sleep disorder. For him, REM sleep paralysis doesn't kick in. The brain's messages for movement, which normally don't reach people's arms and legs during dreams, actually **do** get there. That means the person can walk, run, dive, or do just about anything. So when the sleeper dreams he is running to jump onto a moving train, he will run and fling himself onto whatever is near him.

People with REM sleep disorder don't act out every dream — perhaps only one every few months. Some dreams involve harmless activities, but the dreams can be violent. People with REM sleep disorder often end up with broken bones, cuts and bruises.

How can you get rid of a nightmare that keeps coming back? Give this a try.

1. Write down everything you can remember about the nightmare.

2. Think up a happy ending.

3. In your mind, go over your dream with its new happy ending. Describe it to someone else or try writing it down. Think about it before you go to bed.

Tossing and Turning

Almost everyone has insomnia (in-SOM-nee-yuh) — trouble sleeping — once in a while. If you're worried about a test, upset with a friend or excited about a trip, your mind may be too busy thinking about it to sleep. Once the problem or event passes, so does the insomnia. Some people, however, have insomnia almost every night, and they may need a doctor's help to solve their sleep problems.

Insomnia isn't the only problem that can keep you tossing and turning. Imagine lying in bed ready to sleep. Just as you relax, you feel a creepy, prickly feeling in the calves of your legs — like ants marching up and down your skin. The feeling gets worse and worse until you can't stand it. You have to get up and walk around.

Ah, relief! But when you lie back down, the creeping returns. Finally, after hours of frustration, you fall asleep. That's what bedtime can be like for the ten percent of people who have Restless Legs Syndrome.

Many people with Restless Legs also have a disorder called Periodic Limb Movements in Sleep (PLMS). While they're asleep, their legs suddenly start jerking a couple of times every minute. Each jerk comes exactly the same number of seconds after the last. Although they don't remember the jerks, each one wakes them up slightly, and in the morning they feel exhausted. PLMS is most common in people over 65, but some younger adults and children have it as well.

Snoring the Night Away

It's night, thousands of years ago. Some early humans are asleep in a cave. A predator smells them and prepares to attack. Suddenly, a loud snore echoes through the cave. The predator hesitates, then decides to look for less dangerous prey. Snoring may have protected our ancient ancestors from fearsome creatures, but today, for most people, it's just a bothersome nighttime noise.

Over 25 percent of men and 15 percent of women snore every night. When a snorer takes a breath, his tongue, his uvula (that thing you see hanging in your throat) and parts of his throat vibrate. All these vibrations make that familiar raspy sound.

Very loud snoring may be a sign of a serious problem called obstructive sleep apnea. An apnea sufferer may stop breathing for up to 60 seconds before he gasps and snorts himself awake enough to take a breath. Some people do this hundreds of times a night, but they don't remember and have no idea why they are so sleepy during the day. Being tired isn't the only problem. The lack of oxygen during the night makes the sleeper's heart work harder and can cause high blood pressure and even a heart attack or stroke.

Not all snorers are in danger. As long as the snoring is steady with no long pauses or snorts, the snorer probably doesn't have obstructive sleep apnea.

- The loudest snore ever recorded reached 93 decibels. That's as loud as an electric blender, a ringing alarm clock or a dog barking just an arm's length away from you.

Sleepwalkers ◆ ◆ ◆

It was the middle of the night when an 11-year-old boy got up out of his bed. He headed for the front door and opened it. And then he was gone. The next morning, his parents were astonished to find his bed empty — and even more surprised when he turned up unharmed 160 km (100 mi.) from home! Was he kidnapped? Did he run away? No, he was sleepwalking. He walked from the house to the nearby railway tracks and climbed aboard a train that carried him out of town.

About 3 kids out of every 20 sleepwalk at least once. Most outgrow it by the time they're 14. Sleepwalking usually happens in the first two hours of the night, during deep sleep (Stage 3 or 4). Some sleepers just sit up in bed. Others walk around. Their eyes are open, but they're not aware of people around them. They often go back to bed after wandering around for up to 30 minutes, and they don't remember a thing about it in the morning. Most sleepwalkers are so deeply asleep, it's best not to try to wake them.

••• Sleeptalkers

What do sleeptalkers talk about? Probably not their dreams, since sleeptalking almost never occurs during REM sleep. Often a person listening to a sleeptalker can't make out any real words. It's usually just muttering and mumbo-jumbo. Many adults talk in their sleep, and even more children do. If you talk to a child shortly after she falls asleep, she will probably say something. If two children share a bedroom, the sound of one of them sleeptalking will sometimes get the other talking, too. Of course, you couldn't call it a conversation since neither has a clue what the other is saying!

Don't step on the frog

Your nose looks like a banana

- **Gorillas who have learned sign language have been known to make signs for words while they are asleep.**

Walks on the Wild Side

Most sleepwalkers end up back in bed. But some don't. Sleepwalkers have been found the next morning snoozing in the bathtub or under the kitchen table. One man went to bed in his room at a hotel and woke to find himself downstairs in the lobby in his pajamas.

Sleepwalking can also involve more than just walking. Sleepwalkers sometimes look through drawers, get dressed or even take down curtains. It's very common for sleepwalking children to walk to a garbage pail, toy box or other object that reminds them of a toilet and — ahem — use it!

Sleep Attack!

A fisherman out on his boat settled into a routine. He cast the line, waited, reeled it in, cast the line again. Then he got a nibble. But before he could reel in his catch, he fell asleep. With a mighty tug, the fish pulled him right out of the boat into the water!

It sounds strange for a person to fall asleep in the middle of doing something, but it happens all the time to people who have narcolepsy (NAR-ko-lep-see). This sleep disorder makes people fall asleep two, three or even twenty times each day, even if they've slept eight or more hours the night before. A sleep attack can overtake them when they're doing almost anything and can last anywhere from 30 seconds to 30 minutes.

People with narcolepsy usually start having sleep attacks as teenagers, but some children have attacks as well. No one really knows why narcolepsy happens. Part of the answer may be that the sleep of these people isn't the same as that of regular sleepers. Narcolepsy sufferers don't drift down through Stages 1 to 4 of non-REM sleep, like most people do. Instead, they go directly into REM sleep and move on to the other stages later in their sleep cycle.

Attacked by Atonia

Many people with narcolepsy also have to cope with cataplexy (CA-tuh-pleks-ee). Remember atonia, the paralysis that takes over your body during REM sleep? In most people with narcolepsy, that paralysis can suddenly be triggered even when they're awake. This creates cataplectic attacks. Whenever the person has strong emotions — for some, happiness or excitement; for others, anger or surprise — their muscles go limp. They may even collapse on the ground and lie there for a few minutes, awake but with their arms and legs completely paralyzed.

- **Ever heard of sleeping sickness? It's a tropical disease that makes you feel tired all the time. It's caused by a parasite that gets into your bloodstream, usually from the bite of a tsetse fly.**
  - **Some animals have narcolepsy, too. Stanford University researchers even bred a whole kennel of narcoleptic dobermans so that they could study them.**

Sitting Bull

In 1977, the bull-fighting industry in Spain had a big problem. Bulls would charge in to the arena — and fall down. Then they'd get up — and fall down again. The fans were outraged.

Eventually, the organizers stopped using the falling-down bulls to breed new ones, and the problem disappeared. Quite likely, the bulls had narcolepsy and were having cataplectic attacks due to the excitement of the fight.

A Good Night's Sleep

When's the last time you complained about your bedtime? Last night? It just never seems fair that kids have to go to sleep while adults stay up later. Unfortunately for kids, the grown-ups have scientific research backing them up. Generally, the younger you are the more sleep you need to keep your growing body and your developing brain working well. If you don't get enough sleep, you'll feel cranky and unhappy, be more likely to get sick and have a much harder time learning new things.

As people get older, their need for sleep drops. But there's one big exception. For reasons doctors and scientists don't completely understand yet, many teenagers seem to need more sleep than they did at age 11 — perhaps because of the major changes their bodies go through at puberty.

How much sleep is enough?	
Age	Hours of sleep needed a day
1 week	16 to 18 hours
1 year	12 to 14 hours
5 years	10 to 12 hours
7 years	9 to 11 hours
11 years	8 to 10 hours
teenager	9 to 10 hours
adult	7 to 9 hours

Lots of people don't get enough sleep. Doctors, firefighters, police officers and many others often go a full day and night with no sleep at all. You'd think they'd feel drowsy but an emergency or an interesting activity can keep even very overtired people awake and alert.

In 1965, a San Diego high school student named Randy Gardner stayed awake for 264 hours — 11 days — to set a new record. Even when he was at his sleepiest, playing some basketball was enough to wake him right up.

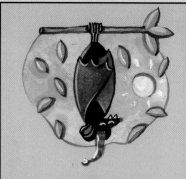

- **Not all animals need the same amount of sleep. Giraffes and elephants get along with only 3 hours, while pet cats sleep 16 hours and bats sleep 20 hours.**

You Try It

Are you getting enough sleep? Try this experiment between 2 P.M. and 4 P.M. to help you find out. Challenge others in your family to try it, too.

1. Sit comfortably in an armchair with one arm over the side. Make sure there are no loud noises, people or other distractions near you.

2. Place a plate on the floor below your hand.

3. Hold a spoon loosely in that hand.

4. Check the time, then relax and try to sleep.

5. If you fall asleep, your hand will relax and the spoon will clatter onto the plate, waking you up. Check the time.

The quicker you fell asleep, the more nighttime sleep you should be getting. If you're still awake with spoon in hand after 20 minutes, you're probably getting the right amount of sleep each night.

Sleeping in Strange Places

Where's the strangest place a person could sleep? Space is definitely high on the list. Astronauts orbiting Earth tuck themselves into a sort of sleeping bag hanging from the shuttle wall, or a tiny cubicle the size of a coffin. Since there's no gravity, they don't quite feel like they're lying down. For one thing, their arms keep floating up in front of their faces! No wonder most astronauts lose between one and three hours of sleep each night that they're in space.

In Your Own Bed

Most people sleep best in familiar surroundings. Lying down in your own bed seems to let you relax more completely and get enough deep sleep, the kind that helps you feel rested and refreshed.

Changing beds or even sleeping positions can make a big difference. For example, ever try to sleep sitting up? Chances are you got very little deep sleep. Your brain knows when you're upright. In fact, it may be trying to protect you by keeping you from relaxing completely so that you won't fall down and hurt yourself.

- **Lions prefer to sleep on their backs.**

- **Leopards sleep in a tree, straddling a branch. Bats sleep upside down, clinging to a tree branch or the ceiling of a cave with the claws of their feet.**

- **Sea otters sometimes sleep floating on their backs in water, clutching a water plant between their paws as an anchor.**

Do you sleep better when everything is familiar? Ask a parent to check on you two nights in a row (about every five minutes or so) to see how long it takes you to fall asleep. The first night, sleep the way you usually do. The next night, follow the same bedtime routine, but change WHERE you sleep — maybe switch beds or sleep with your head at the foot end. Did you fall asleep as quickly the second night?

Famous Sleepers

The inventor Thomas Edison thought sleep was a huge waste of time. He believed that if he conquered darkness, he could free up many hours for work. In a way, he was right. In 1910, before Edison invented the lightbulb, young adults slept about nine hours each night. Now, thanks to Edison's lightbulb, people stay up longer and sleep only seven hours a night. That means adults are awake for about 700 more hours each year.

Edison himself claimed he slept only four hours a night. But he often took two naps of three hours each during the day. Experts say the naps boosted his creativity and probably helped him invent the very thing that keeps the rest of us awake. In fact, they say napping for as little as 20 minutes can improve a person's abilities for the next 10 hours.

- Animals nap, too. Some birds take mini naps of 30 seconds or so while flying. That's how they manage to fly non-stop during long migrations.

- Porpoises and bottle-nosed dolphins breathe air, yet sleep underwater. At night, half their brain stays alert enough to get them to the surface to breathe. Every two hours or so through the night, the sleeping side of the brain awakes and the other side gets its chance to sleep.

Notable Nappers

The French Emperor Napoleon Bonaparte always went to bed at 10 P.M., but was usually up again by 2 A.M. He'd work at his desk until 5 A.M. and then nap until 7 A.M. Winston Churchill, the former British prime minister, did almost the opposite. He usually worked late, until 3 or 4 A.M., and then slept until 8 A.M. Then he took a two-hour nap in the afternoon.

Leonardo da Vinci, the famous artist and scientist, may have been the most interesting napper. According to folklore, he never got a full night's sleep. He just napped for 15 minutes every four hours — a total of just one and a half hours of sleep a day! Experiments have shown that da Vinci's 90 minutes of sleep aren't enough to survive on for more than three or four days. Still, da Vinci may have used this napping strategy when he was racing to finish a project, such as when he was dissecting human bodies to study anatomy. He would've had just three or four days to dissect a body before it became badly decomposed.

Not all famous thinkers are nappers. The brilliant scientist Albert Einstein loved to sleep. He said he was at his best only when he got 10 hours of sleep a night.

Larks and Owls

Most adults go to sleep between 10 P.M. and midnight and wake up between 6 and 7:30 A.M. But some people, nicknamed "larks," feel tired shortly after supper. They go to bed early and rise the next morning with the sun, full of energy. Other people are called "owls" because they stay up late and don't feel fully awake until mid-morning.

Index